THE STORY OF

FREDERICK DOUGLASS,
Voice of Freedom

BY ERIC WEINER

ILLUSTRATED BY STEVEN PARTON

A YEARLING BOOK

ABOUT THIS BOOK

The events described in this book are true. They have been carefully researched and excerpted from authentic autobiographies, writings, and commentaries. No part of this biography has been fictionalized. To learn more about Frederick Douglass, ask your librarian to recommend other fine books you might read.

To my parents

Published by
Dell Publishing
a division of
Bantam Doubleday Dell Publishing Group, Inc.
666 Fifth Avenue
New York, New York 10103

ISBN: 0-440-40560-2

Published by arrangement with Parachute Press, Inc.
Printed in the United States of America
February 1992
10 9 8 7 6 5 4 3 2 1
OPM

Contents

Introduction

That morning the six-year-old boy woke up to the sound of a woman screaming.

The boy was a slave, so he wasn't allowed to sleep in a bed. He tried to stay warm by sleeping in a sack on the floor of the kitchen closet.

On cold nights, he almost froze. The soles of his feet cracked in the cold. And then, that morning, he heard the horrifying screams.

Through the cracks in the closet door, the boy could see into the kitchen. Terrified, he now watched as the Old Master dragged a slave woman into the room. He tied her hands to a hook in the ceiling.

It was Esther. She had disobeyed an order from the master. And she had been caught.

He would teach her a lesson for disobeying his orders, the master shouted. He took a strip of cowskin and whipped her back until it bled.

Esther was screaming. But he didn't stop.

1

Watching from the closet, the boy shook with terror. The whipping seemed to go on forever. Finally, the master let the woman go. The kitchen was quiet again. But the boy didn't come out. He was sure the master would whip him next. He stayed hidden in the closet for hours.

He wasn't whipped. Not this time. But the little boy had learned an awful lesson. He now knew what poor Esther had learned long ago. Life as a slave was a life of terror. Being a slave meant being helpless. There was no way the slaves could defend themselves.

All the older slaves knew this only too well. But there was something that the slaves and their masters did not know. Nobody knew that someday this little boy was going to grow up and change all that.

The young boy's name was Frederick. One day, Frederick Douglass would help to set his entire people free.

The Long Journey

Grandmamma's hut had a dirt floor. There were no windows, just holes cut in the logs. Freddy was four. So far, this was the only home he'd ever known.

He had been born here in Tuckahoe, Maryland, in February, 1818. His full name was Frederick Augustus Washington Bailey. His mother and grandmother were slaves as well. In fact, his family probably had been slaves in Tuckahoe for over a hundred years.

Slave traders had been stealing African people out of their homes since the 1500s. Thousands and thousands of slaves were brought to the southern part of the U.S. after 1619 and put to work on farms. They had to work from morning till night without pay. Special laws had been passed to preserve this awful system. The law said that the children of slaves would be slaves as well. And the children of the children. And so on—forever.

3

Freddy had been taken away from his mother, Harriet Bailey, when he was just a baby.

She had been sent to work for Mr. Stewart. Mr. Stewart ran another plantation, or huge farm, twelve long miles away from where Freddy now lived with Grandmamma.

Freddy almost never saw his mother. Each day the tall, dark woman worked long, back-breaking hours in the fields. To visit her son, she had to sneak out at night. If she was caught, she would be whipped. She would be sold to owners even farther away. Still, she came whenever she could.

Worn out, she would hike for miles through the darkness. When she reached the hut, she lay down beside the young boy. Freddy would wake up just long enough to give her a hug. When he woke up in the morning, she was always gone.

Still, these first few years with Grandmamma would be some of the only happy times in Frederick's entire childhood.

Fred was a very smart boy. He was capable of entertaining himself. Grandmamma's hut was on the outskirts of the plantation. There were woods all around. Gray squirrels were always scrambling up and down the trees right outside Fred's window. He loved to watch them.

When he ran out of things to do, Freddy tagged after his grandmamma. Grandmamma had

many talents. She was famous among the slaves for her ability to grow sweet potatoes. She was said to have a magical touch that made things grow.

Grandmamma was excellent at fishing. She made her own nets. While Fred played on the bank, she'd wade into the water up to her waist. She fished for hours, catching shad and herring. Fred wanted to be like his tall, strong grandmamma in every way.

Fred always listened carefully when he heard the grown-ups talking. One day, he learned something that scared him very much. He found out that Grandmamma's hut didn't belong to her. It belonged to someone called the "Old Master."

Not only that, Grandmamma herself belonged to the Old Master. And so did Freddy!

It was hard to believe. He was *owned* by somebody, like a chair. When he got older, he would have to go live with his owner.

Freddy was terrified. And when Freddy turned six years old, the dreaded day arrived.

Grandmamma put off telling him for as long as she could. That morning she only told him they were going on a trip.

It was a hot and humid day. Grandmamma lived many miles from the Old Master's house. They would have to travel on foot.

This was a long hike for a six-year-old boy. But

whenever he got too tired, Grandmamma carried him on her shoulders.

Fred tried not to let her carry him too much, though. He wanted to act like a man.

Late in the afternoon Grandmamma and Fred arrived at a huge white house. There were children everywhere. Black, brown, and white. They were all playing together. When they saw Fred, they asked him to join in their games. Fred refused.

Grandmamma was looking very sad. But she patted the top of Fred's head. She told him to be a good boy.

"Go and play with them," Grandmamma said.

She pointed to a black boy. She said this was his older brother, Perry. She pointed to two black girls. These were his sisters, Sarah and Eliza.

Brothers and sisters? Fred had never seen any of them before.

The kids kept asking him to play. So did Grandmamma. But Fred was terrified that his grandmamma would leave him.

He stood with his back to the wall and waited while Grandmamma went into the kitchen. He kept his eye on the kitchen door. He wanted to be sure he knew where she was at all times.

Suddenly, a young girl came running up to him, grinning meanly. "Fed, Fed," she taunted, "Grandmamma gone!"

This couldn't be true. Fred raced into the kitchen.

It was true. There was no Grandmamma in sight. And the little boy fell to the floor, sobbing. But Grandmamma did not return to comfort him. That night Fred cried himself to sleep.

The Life of a Slave

Days passed, and still there was no sign of Grandmamma. Freddy missed her terribly.

Living in Grandmamma's hut, he had felt safe. Now he began to learn about how scary slave life really was.

Fred had no shoes and barely any clothes. None of the slave children did. They ran around almost naked. Fred wore only a coarse sack that reached to his knees, even when it was cold.

As a form of respect, slaves called the elder slaves "Aunt" and "Uncle." The cook was known as Aunt Katy. She was in charge of all of the slave children.

Aunt Katy could be very mean. If Aunt Katy was mad at a child, she wouldn't let that child eat for a day or two at a time.

There wasn't enough food to begin with. Often, Fred was so hungry that he fought over crumbs with Nep, the dog!

Then, one day, Aunt Katy decided to punish Fred. No food all day, she told him. Fred didn't even know what he had done wrong!

He felt all right at first. But by dinnertime he was starving. He watched Aunt Katy use her big knife to cut off pieces of bread for the other children. She wouldn't give Fred any. She told him she planned to starve him to death.

Later that night Fred sat by the kitchen fire. He was too hungry to sleep. But Aunt Katy still wouldn't let him have so much as a scrap.

Then he saw it. On a high shelf in the kitchen lay an ear of Indian corn. He would have to be quick. He knew that if Aunt Katy caught him, she would beat him badly. He waited until Aunt Katy left the room. Then he clambered up and pulled out a few kernels. He roasted the kernels in the fire. Then he began to devour his tiny snack.

Just then, the kitchen door opened. He was caught!

But he wasn't. It wasn't Aunt Katy at all. It was his mother!

Harriet Bailey still worked on Mr. Stewart's plantation. Now that Fred had moved out of Grandmamma's hut, she had walked even farther to reach him. But she had come.

Instantly Fred was in his mother's arms. Why had he been crying, she wanted to know. He told her what Aunt Katy had done. She comforted him with kisses and a ginger cake.

Then Aunt Katy returned. Fred's mother was very angry. She warned Aunt Katy what would happen to her if she ever treated her Fred like this again.

Harriet was not a woman one took lightly. Though she was being kept as a slave, she still managed to keep her great dignity and power.

But in the morning, when Fred woke up, she was gone again.

This was to be her last visit. A year later he got word that his mother was sick. His master refused to let the boy visit her. Then word came that she had died. Fred wasn't even allowed to go to her funeral.

The days passed, and slowly Fred began to adjust to his new life. There were plenty of kids around to play with and a lot to see.

On his master's huge plantation, the slaves grew tobacco, wheat, and corn. There were slaves who worked as shoemakers, blacksmiths, wheelmakers, barrelmakers, weavers, and grain grinders. There were slaves who worked in the fields and slaves who worked as servants in the house. There were slaves in the stable and slaves at the windmill.

Many of the slaves sang while they worked. The slaves made up the words as they went along.

Since the owners might be listening, the words of the song had to be happy words. But the slaves sang the songs sadly. Often, Fred could hear the field hands in the distance.

The mournful songs made Fred feel even sadder. The songs told him that his elders were suffering, too.

Years later Fred would hear people say that the slaves were happy being slaves. "After all," people would say, "they're always singing!"

Fred was amazed. He knew firsthand that slave songs were very sad songs. He never forgot them. In fact, the rich, rolling tones would help Frederick to become a great speaker someday. He would weave his memories of slave life into mighty speeches that were like songs themselves.

But that was far in the future. Right now, Fred was just beginning to understand why the slaves were so unhappy. Each day the slaves were forced to work until it was too dark to see. They had to eat their tiny meals while still at work. Then they had to hurry home to do their own chores.

Then it was time for bed. The overseer's horn would wake them at dawn. The poor slaves needed every little bit of sleep they could get to make it through the next awful day.

The little boy saw one horrifying sight after another. He saw slaves being whipped for the slightest reason. Sometimes slaves were whipped simply for not answering fast enough. Sometimes they were whipped because the master didn't like their expression. Fred was frightened. How could people be treated like this?

Then Fred saw the worst sight of all: murder. A slave dove into the pond to escape being beaten. The overseer told the slave to get out of the water. The slave refused. The overseer warned the slave he would count to three. If the slave wasn't out of the pond by three, he would shoot him dead.

The overseer counted to three. Knee-deep in the water, the slave still didn't move. The overseer pulled out a gun and killed the man on the spot.

The other slaves who saw the murder could do nothing about it, Fred learned. Under the law, blacks had no rights at all. They were considered less than human. They were not even allowed to be witnesses in a trial. Nothing they said would mean anything in court.

This would not be the only murder of a slave that Fred saw or heard about. And the young boy didn't escape punishment himself. He was whipped often. Why?

Fred was feeling more independent than ever. He didn't like to do as he was told. And why should he listen to orders from people who treated their slaves this way? Whenever he disobeyed an order, no matter how slight, he was flogged.

He was nine years old now. At least, he *thought*

he was nine. His owners would never tell him exactly when he was born.

The white children all knew their birthdays. On their birthdays they had parties and got presents. Fred often asked himself why he couldn't have a birthday.

He was angry, and he had lots of questions. He wondered why he was a slave, or why he couldn't live with his own grandmamma.

Fred had seen that a few blacks were free. How could this be? The slaves explained that sometimes a kind master let a grown-up slave have his freedom.

These answers didn't satisfy Fred. But he had no choice. He would have to remain a slave . . . for now.

Fred was still too young to go to work in the fields. His only chores were driving in the cows at night, cleaning up the yard, and running errands for his mistress.

Fred liked the last job best. Miss Lucretia seemed to like him. Sometimes he would stand beneath her window and sing. When he did, she often gave him a piece of bread and butter. Sometimes she smiled at him. For a boy who had lost his mother, these smiles meant a lot.

One day he got into a fight with a boy named

Ike. Ike picked up a piece of iron and smashed Fred in the head.

Bleeding badly, the boy ran to Aunt Katy. But the mean cook would pay no attention.

"It serves you right" was all she said.

Just then, Miss Lucretia called Fred into the parlor. She quietly washed the blood off his forehead. Then she put on some balsam to heal the wound. With her gentle hands, she bound his head in a soft linen cloth.

The wound formed a small white cross on his forehead. For the rest of his life, Fred would bear the scar from this fight.

One day Miss Lucretia called for him. She had some incredible news.

Fred was being sent away. The Old Master had given Fred to a relative of Miss Lucretia's as a gift. This relative was a little boy, younger than Fred. It would be Fred's job to look after him. The little boy's family lived in Baltimore.

Most young boys would be very sad to leave home. But Fred told himself that his new life couldn't be any worse than his life was now.

Fred would leave in three days. He had never been this excited in all his life. At night he couldn't sleep. He was afraid that he would be left behind.

A New Home

That Saturday Fred's master had to send a flock of sheep to Baltimore. Fred was sent along with the sheep. Fred didn't look back. He hoped he would never see the plantation again.

The trip was thrilling. First they passed Annapolis. Fred couldn't believe the size of the dome on the state house building.

On Sunday morning they arrived in Baltimore itself. It was the biggest town Fred had ever seen. The boat docked at Smith's wharf. Now Fred had to help Rich, one of the sailors, drive the sheep to Slater's Hill. Then Rich took the nine-year-old to meet the Aulds. Fred could hardly wait to meet the new family he'd be working for.

The Aulds lived on Alliciana Street, near Gardner's Shipyard. Mr. and Mrs. Auld and their little son Tommy all came to the door to greet the young boy.

Fred couldn't believe what he saw. Mrs. Auld

was smiling at him warmly. Could it be that he had found a home at last?

"Here is your Freddy," the kind-looking woman said to her son. "Fred will take care of you."

Mrs. Auld smiled at Fred and added, "Be kind to little Tommy."

Fred didn't need to be told. He was delighted by his warm greeting. He felt that he already loved the rosy-cheeked young boy. Suddenly he had a new father, mother, and younger brother. For one brief moment the little boy felt as if everything would be all right.

For a country boy, Baltimore took some getting used to. It was summer, and hot. The tall buildings crowded him in and made him feel even hotter. The brick sidewalks burned his bare feet. The noise and bustle of the city scared him. Sometimes Fred almost wished he were back in the country on the Tuckahoe plantation.

But not quite. For the first time in his life, Fred had real clothes to wear. Instead of the cold closet floor, he now slept on a rug. Instead of fighting with the dog for crumbs of cornmeal, he now ate good bread and mush.

And most importantly, he felt as if he had a mother.

Mrs. Auld's first name was Sophia. Fred called her "Miss Sopha." She had never owned a slave before. She treated him as a human being, not a piece of property.

When she bounced Tommy on her knee, she let Freddy stand by her side. When she wasn't holding Tommy, she let the older boy rest his head in her lap. Fred was starved for affection.

On the plantation Fred had been taught never to look a white person in the eye. That showed disrespect, he was told. He must always hang his head and mumble.

But Miss Sopha had a completely different manner. To Fred, her warm smile seemed to say: "Look up, child. Don't be afraid."

Her husband, Hugh Auld, wasn't as friendly. The shipbuilder looked like a sour and scary person. But even Mr. Auld smiled at him sometimes.

And so, at first, everything went well. Fred took care of Tommy. He was so excited to be out of Tuckahoe, he did all his chores happily.

Miss Sopha was a religious woman. Fred often heard her reading the Bible aloud. This made him curious. How does a person read?

Fred had never had a school lesson in his life. His owners had worked hard to keep the slaves from getting any education. Now he wondered how Miss Sopha could tell what words to say just by looking at those marks on the page.

Miss Sopha appeared to be so friendly, Fred dared to ask her. Would she teach him how to read?

To his amazement, his mistress agreed. She would be happy to teach him!

Fred was extremely smart. He learned very quickly. Miss Sopha was amazed. People said slaves were stupid. But soon Fred knew the entire alphabet and could even spell a few three-letter words.

Fred felt proud. Miss Sopha felt even prouder. She was sure that her husband would be delighted with the news. In front of Fred, she told Mr. Auld about the lessons. She bragged about how smart Fred was.

But Mr. Auld was not delighted. He was furious. He ordered her to stop the lessons at once. He said it was against the law to teach a slave to read.

"If you give a slave an inch, he'll take a mile," he ranted. "A slave should know nothing but to obey his master—to do as he is told to do."

Miss Sopha protested, but Mr. Auld went on: "If you teach that slave how to read, there will be no keeping him."

Mr. Auld made Miss Sopha promise never to teach Fred again. Miss Sopha agreed.

In a way, this could have been a terrible setback for Fred. But it wasn't. Fred had heard every word Mr. Auld had said. The words had sunk in deep. *If you teach that slave how to read, there will be no keeping him.*

His master's angry words brought Fred to a

shocking realization. Mr. Auld was afraid that Fred would stop being a slave. That he would somehow find his freedom. If Mr. Auld was afraid, then freedom must be possible!

The boy had never dared to believe such a thing. It was hard to imagine. If he were free, he would no longer have to take orders. He would be a real person, not a piece of property. He could stand up for himself. People couldn't punish him whenever they felt like it.

Perhaps he could also free his own family. Then he could live with his grandmamma again! He would go to school like white children did—and he would be taught to read and write. When he grew up, he could get a job!

It all sounded like an impossible dream. But what Mr. Auld had said made him think there was a way. And if there was a way, Freddy told himself, he would find it. For the first time, he had a goal in life. He told himself that nothing could stop him now. Somehow, some way, he would learn how to read.

New Friends

Miss Sopha's kindness toward Fred had come to an end. Perhaps she still felt affection for the boy. But if she did, she bent over backward not to show it. Mr. Auld had given her his orders, and she was determined to carry them out.

Every chance Fred got, he would study a newspaper or book. He was trying to practice his alphabet. But whenever Miss Sopha caught him, she flew into a fury. She warned him never to do it again.

If Fred stayed out of sight for too long, she would send for him. She would demand to know what he had been doing.

But Fred was even more determined than she was. He took his punishment quietly. It made him mad, but he tried not to show it. No matter how much trouble he got into, no matter how badly he was punished, he would learn to read.

Whenever Fred was sent on an errand, he hid *Webster's Spelling Book* and some bread in his pocket.

He would run the errand as quickly as he could. He didn't have much time to spare. If he took too long coming back home, he would get in terrible trouble. But each time he stopped to pay a special visit.

There was a group of poor white boys who often gathered on a corner in his neighborhood. Fred had made friends with them. Most whites didn't like to be seen spending time with lowly black slaves. But this group of boys wasn't like that. They liked Fred and were always glad to see him. Their kindness meant a great deal to him. He never forgot their names as long as he lived: they were Gustavus Dorgan, Joseph Bailey, Charles Farity, and William Cosdry.

Sometimes Fred talked to the boys about slavery. He tried out his ideas on his new friends. When they were grown-up, they could do whatever they wanted, he said. But not him. He would be a slave for life. Didn't he have the same rights as every human being? Didn't he deserve to be free? Why would God make someone a slave?

His friends looked troubled. Then they all agreed! They tried to console Fred. They told him they were sure he would be free someday. They told him not to give up hope.

It was an incredible feeling. He had tried out his secret ideas about slavery, and they had worked. People had agreed with him.

Now Fred took out his spelling book and the

bread. He offered the bread to any boy who would give him a spelling lesson.

He found the boys were glad to teach him. And slowly, letter by letter, Fred began to learn how to read.

But his lessons were few and far between. And Miss Sopha kept a close watch on the boy at home. Learning to read would take Fred four long years.

Fred was twelve years old now and getting closer to his goal. He was reading better and faster all the time. Then one day a letter arrived from Tuckahoe. Freddy's Old Master had died. He died without writing a will. That meant he didn't say who would get his possessions. By law, one of his possessions was Fred.

The master's family ordered Fred to return at once. The master's property was going to be divided among his children.

That was that. One letter, and Freddy was ripped right out of his home in Baltimore.

Fred was terrified. He prayed that at least he would be given to Lucretia. Maybe Lucretia would be kind enough to return him to Baltimore. But it was just as possible that he would be sold to someone new. There was no way to tell.

Fred knew that, for a slave, he had so far been very lucky. He lived in Maryland, one of the most northern of the slave states. In the states just to the north, blacks were free! Perhaps because it was close to the North, Maryland treated its slaves better than the Deep South.

What if Fred was sold to an owner in Georgia or Mississippi? He tried not to picture what would happen to him.

The time came to say good-bye to Tommy and Miss Sopha. When Tommy said good-bye, he started to cry. So did Miss Sopha. Fred began to cry as well.

Within a few days he was back in Tuckahoe. Here he learned that all the slaves were hoping to be given to Lucretia. Fred quickly found out why.

On the day he arrived, Freddy stood talking with his brother Perry. He didn't really know the boy. Fred hadn't seen him in years. Suddenly Master Andrew stormed in.

Earlier, Perry had gone off to play. While he was gone, the master had wanted him to run an errand. The boy was supposed to be available to the master at all times. When the master couldn't find Perry, he flew into a rage. Now he grabbed Perry by the throat, threw him down to the ground, and stomped on his head with the heel of his boot.

Blood was pouring out of Perry's nose and ears. Freddy stared at Master Andrew in horror and amazement.

Master Andrew sneered at Fred. He said he would do the same to him someday soon, as soon as Fred belonged to him.

The day for dividing up the property arrived. The inspectors made all the slaves line up. They had to line up next to the pigs, the cattle, and the sheep. Each one was inspected along with the animals.

The inspectors examined each person roughly. They wanted to see how strong and healthy each one was. They would decide how many dollars each human being was worth.

Fred waited anxiously to find out who his new owner would be. At last the word came. He would be given to Lucretia! Not only that, she said she would send him back to live with the Aulds.

Soon Fred was on his way back to Baltimore. But just one month later, Lucretia died. Fred's ownership was passed on to Lucretia's husband, Thomas. Fred knew, if Thomas wanted, he could be called back to the plantation at Tuckahoe at any time. Fred prayed this wouldn't happen. Thomas was a dangerous man to work for.

Fred's poor Grandmamma was in danger, too. Grandmamma had slaved for the Old Master's family all her life. She had rocked the master when he was a baby. She had raised slave child after child for him, only to see them sold like sheep. When the

master died, she hadn't been lucky like Fred. Instead of being given to Lucretia, Grandmamma was given to the master's son, Andrew.

Grandmamma was blind now and couldn't do any more work. So Andrew took her out of her hut. He put her in a much smaller hut, way off in the woods. If she could find food to eat, fine. If she couldn't, that was also fine with Andrew. He was leaving Grandmamma to die.

Grandmamma had given Fred his only happy years. But she was still in Tuckahoe and Fred was in Baltimore. There was nothing he could do to help her.

Magic Words

Fred remained upset about one particular thing. He still didn't know when his birthday was. He tried to keep track of time as best he could. He figured he was thirteen now. He could now read as well as any other child, including white children who had gone to school. He read so well that he was giving reading lessons to other black slaves. These lessons had to be secret, of course. He wasn't supposed to know how to read himself, let alone teach others.

But Fred remembered Mr. Auld's warning. Teach a slave to read and he might become free. Fred told himself that the more slaves who knew how to read, the better.

He himself was dying to read anything he could get his hands on. But Miss Sopha wouldn't let him even glance at a book or a paper. Sometimes Fred found pages of the Bible lying in the gutter. These he would carefully clean, dry, and study.

In a nearby house lived a slave named Uncle Lawson. Uncle Lawson loved the Bible with a great passion, but he couldn't read as well as Fred. So whenever he could, Fred would visit Uncle Lawson and give him reading lessons.

In return, Uncle Lawson told Fred stories from the Bible. He taught Fred about religion.

Uncle Lawson said it was man who had made Fred a slave. But God had very important work in mind for Fred. It was up to Fred to prepare himself for this work.

Uncle Lawson's ideas made Fred feel wonderful. The thought that God didn't want him to be a slave gave him strength. He began to daydream about what his great work might be. Maybe someday he would lead his people!

Fred knew if he was going to get anywhere, he would have to educate himself first. That meant he would need reading material. He came up with a plan. Miss Sopha kept a close watch on him at home. His only freedom came when she sent him to run an errand.

In the course of Fred's errands, he sometimes had a chance to earn some money. He would offer to shine a rich gentleman's shoes. As a slave, he was required to turn over any money he earned to his master. But now Fred secretly kept the pennies for himself.

Eventually, he had saved up fifty cents! It was

just enough for what Fred wanted. He took the money to Thames Street and bought a popular book of stories and poems called the *The Columbian Orator*. At last he had something to read!

He kept the book hidden from his mistress. He read it whenever he found time. In the *Orator,* he came upon a remarkable story.

The story was about a master and a slave. The slave kept running away. After catching him for a second time, the master was very angry. He pointed out all the ways he had been kind to the slave. Why, he asked, was the slave so ungrateful?

In response, the slave gave a long speech. He talked about the evils of slavery. He said that no man had the right to own another person. He talked about some of the awful ways he had suffered.

The master was upset and moved by his slave's speech. He was so moved that he let the slave go free.

Fred couldn't believe it. Here, in this book, were some of the exact same things he had thought all along! He wasn't the only one who thought that slavery was wrong. Many other people agreed with him! They had written about it in a *book*. This convinced Fred that his private ideas weren't just crazy notions. They were real.

Fred had rarely heard anyone say a bad word about slavery. He had felt as if he were all alone against the world. But now he knew better. And he was going to find out even more.

Mr. Auld was right. Learning to read *was* a powerful thing. Fred had made up his mind. He would not stay a slave for life. Someday he would escape and go free.

Fred was thrilled by his new power. He read everything he could get his hands on—newspapers, the Bible, Shakespeare.

Fred had often heard white people talking angrily about the "abolitionists." *Abolitionist?* It was a long, hard word. Fred had no idea what it meant. But when white people mentioned it, they got very angry. They cursed and talked about the slaves. If the word "abolitionist" made slave owners mad, Fred was sure it meant something good for him.

He watched for his chance. When no one was looking, he snuck over to the dictionary and looked it up.

Abolition, said the dictionary, was the act of abolishing.

What did that mean? In the local newspaper, *The Baltimore American*, Fred finally found the answer.

A group of *abolitionists* had asked the United States Congress to pass a new law. The abolitionists wanted Congress to outlaw the trading of slaves between the states. This was just the beginning. Someday they hoped to abolish slavery itself.

To abolish meant to do away with. Now Fred knew. There was a group of people, white and black, who were trying to do away with slavery!

Fred had some slave friends whom he trusted. He asked them about the abolitionists. He learned that this movement was growing stronger every day. There was even an "underground railroad" that helped slaves escape to the North. It wasn't a real railroad. Slaves hid in people's houses as they traveled north. These houses were known as "stations."

One slave, Nat Turner, had tried something even more daring. He had led a slave rebellion! The rebellion had failed, but the struggle against slavery continued.

More than ever, Fred thought about running away. He knew that if he was caught, the punishment would be severe. But if he could somehow make it all the way to a Northern state like New York, then he would be free.

But how? How did slaves find the underground railroad? And how did they make it from house to house?

In those days, African-Americans could not travel anywhere without special passes. Any white person had the right to stop a black traveler. They could demand to see his or her traveling papers.

Many white people preyed on the defenseless blacks. If they caught an escaped slave, they collected a reward. And even if black people had the proper traveling papers, they weren't safe. Kidnappers could rip up their papers. Then they'd sell the blacks as slaves in another state.

Still, Fred told himself, he would need traveling papers if he was ever going to get free. Then he had a new idea. If only he could somehow learn to *write*. Then he could write out a fake pass.

Mr. Auld often sent Freddy on errands to the shipyard. There, carpenters were always busy, building new ships. Fred saw that the carpenters wrote letters on the timber. They marked each piece of wood to show what part of the ship it was for. Wood for the starboard forward side of the ship was marked "S.F." Wood for the larboard aft side was marked "L.A."

When the carpenters went to lunch, Fred had to stay behind and serve as a watchboy. He was glad to be left alone. As soon as everyone left, he went to work. He copied out the carpenters' letters again and again and again.

Soon he could make these four letters perfectly. "If I can make four letters, I can make more," he promised himself.

Fred's old white friends Gustavus and Charles had moved away. He couldn't find new boys who were willing to teach him to read. Fred had to trick them into giving him lessons.

Whenever Fred ran into a boy who could write, he would brag that he could write just as well.

"I don't believe you," the boy would say. "Let me see you try it."

"S.F.L.A.," Fred would write. Then he'd say, "Beat that."

Showing off, the boy would write out several more letters. And Fred would learn.

He took to carrying a lump of chalk in his pocket. He practiced his writing wherever he could. He chalked letters onto the pavement, fences, and brick walls.

All this time, young Tommy had been going to school. Tommy was being taught to read and write. One day Fred came across some of Tommy's old notebooks. Here were *all* the letters, written out.

Every Monday afternoon Fred was left alone in the house. He always used the time for the same thing. He took the notebook and filled in his letters right under Tommy's. If he was caught, he would be whipped. But he kept at it until he had learned how to write.

The Camp Meeting

Three years had passed. Fred was fifteen now. His life was about to take another turn for the worse.

His real owner, Master Thomas, had gotten into an argument with Master Hugh, the man Fred was loaned to in Baltimore. To punish Hugh, Thomas decided to bring Fred back to Tuckahoe. In just a few days, Fred was shipped back to work on the plantation.

Thomas soon proved to be a cruel and horrible master. He whipped Fred often. His new wife, Rowena, was cruel, too. Fred and the other slaves were kept starving while the cupboard stayed full of extra food.

After a few months with Thomas, Fred was desperate. He couldn't stand being a slave any longer. He made up his mind to try an escape—even if it cost him his life.

But just then, a religious group came to town.

They were holding what was known as a camp meeting.

In a camp meeting, traveling preachers visited small country towns and set up a stage. The meeting went on for days. People came from miles around to hear the preachers talk about God. Some of these people didn't live near a church. The camp meeting was their first chance to be introduced to religion.

Master Thomas had never believed in religion before. But he decided to go to the camp meeting. That excited Fred. Maybe Thomas would find out that God was against slavery, as Uncle Lawson had once explained to him.

At the meeting Fred saw that the visitors had set up tents around the stage, in row after row. That way, they could keep their places overnight. People who couldn't afford tents sat in their wagons and ox carts.

But there were no seats at all for the black people. If they wanted to watch, they had to stand behind the stage. That's where Fred stood.

Fred watched Master Thomas listen to the sermons. Thanks to the camp meeting, he became religious. Thomas and his wife began to pray often. They sang loud hymns morning and night. The house was always filled with preachers.

But Thomas and Rowena still didn't give the

slaves enough to eat. They didn't treat Fred any better than they had before.

Even though he had become religious, Master Thomas didn't stop whipping his slaves. Instead he read to the slaves from the Bible while he whipped them!

Fred was stunned. Clearly, Fred thought, Master Thomas didn't understand God's will. Fred remembered what Uncle Lawson had taught him. God wanted Master Thomas to be good to all people, not just the whites.

It was a bitter lesson. He had learned that it wasn't enough for a person to *act* religious. People could pretend without really changing their ways.

No other slave Fred knew could read and write. He wanted to spread his knowledge to his people, no matter what the risk. He wanted to teach his people what he believed about God. Soon after the camp meeting, Fred started to teach his own secret Sunday school. The class met at the home of a freed slave, James Mitchell.

His school didn't last long. At the second meeting Master Thomas and some other men burst in. They had sticks and other weapons. They beat the students and drove them away. The men warned Fred not to try anything like this again.

Fred was amazed all over again. How could

Master Thomas think he was religious, when he was willing to beat other people to keep them from praying to God?

He didn't have an answer. And Master Thomas had taken to beating him often and brutally.

He was also starving. Desperate for food, the teenager found a trick for getting something to eat. He would let the master's horse run free. The horse always ran down the road several miles to Mr. Hamilton's farm, which bordered on Thomas's. There, the horse knew, there were good oats to eat.

Fred liked Hamilton's farm for the same reason. He had made friends with Aunt Mary, Mr. Hamilton's slave cook. The cook would give Fred scraps of food.

Every time Fred tried this trick, he was whipped. But he didn't stop. He had to eat.

At last, Master Thomas gave up. He told Fred he was going to send him to Edward Covey.

Covey was a neighbor of Master Thomas's. He made a living farming and "breaking in" unruly slaves. They said he could break the spirit of any man.

Master Thomas said he was sending Fred to Edward Covey for a whole year. "To be broken," he said.

The Fight

It was a freezing morning in January. The starving boy had to walk the seven miles to Mr. Covey's farm.

Fred knew that life with Covey would be bad. He was scared. But at least, he told himself, there might be food to eat. That was all he could hope for.

Mr. Covey ran a huge farm. The slaves he was "breaking" did all the work. For the first time in his life, Fred would have to work as a field hand.

He had heard that this was the worst job a slave could have. He soon found out that this was true.

At the crack of dawn, the overseer blew his horn. All the slaves had to rush out of bed. Anyone who was even a second late getting up was whipped. The slaves worked every day until it was too dark to see.

Fred was only with Covey three days before he

got his first beating. At sunrise Mr. Covey ordered Fred to fetch a huge pile of wood from the forest. He gave the boy a pair of huge, wild oxen to help him drag the wood. If the oxen start to run, Covey said, Fred should just pull on the rope and yell "Whoa!"

As soon as Covey left, the powerful beasts began to grunt and snort. They broke into a run. They dragged Fred along at the end of the rope!

He was able to keep up with the oxen until they got to the woods. But now they were pulling him right into the trees. At last Fred got the oxen to stop. He loaded the wood. He almost made it back to the farm safely. Just before he reached the gate, the oxen broke into a run again. They crashed into the fence. It splintered, and Fred was almost crushed to death.

He had come within inches of being killed. But he was only worried about Covey.

Covey walked over and stared at the broken gate. His green eyes looked ferocious. "Go back to the woods again," he said.

Fred pulled on the rope and led the oxen back toward the woods. Covey followed behind him.

When they reached the woods, Covey ordered Fred to stop the cart. He would teach Fred never to break a gate again, he said. The farmer cut down a long branch of black gum tree with his jackknife.

These branches were so tough they were used to whip the big oxen. He ordered Fred to take off his clothes.

Fred didn't answer and he didn't move. Covey ordered him again.

"If you will beat me," Fred said to himself, "you will do so over my clothes."

Again Covey gave the order. When Fred didn't answer, Covey rushed at him. He beat the boy with all his might.

This wasn't the worst beating Fred got. Covey was always finding new reasons to whip his slaves. Sometimes he would pretend to leave the field where slaves were working. Then he would double back and surprise them. If a slave wasn't working hard enough, he would get a whipping.

Fred knew that it was Covey's job to break him in. He felt as if Covey was succeeding. He was always so tired. He never had the strength to read. All thoughts of escaping had vanished. He could barely think.

But the worst was yet to come.

Fred had now been working for Covey for seven long, horrible months. It was a scorching day in August. Covey worked Fred so hard that he fainted.

The farmer kicked the fallen slave with all his might. He told him to get up. Fred tried to get to his feet, but he fell back down again. Covey kicked him some more. Fred managed to stand up this time. But after a few steps he fell back down.

Covey picked up a large piece of wood. "If you have got a headache, I'll cure you," he said. He slammed the wood down on Fred's head. "Now get up," he commanded.

But it was no use. Fred knew he couldn't get up. He told himself if Covey killed him, it was meant to be. He was as good as dead anyway. He was too sick to move. It was the lowest moment of his life. He had lost all will to live.

Covey finally gave up. He stopped kicking Fred. He left the young man lying in the dirt and went back to work.

Fred lay in the dust for a long time. The pain in his head was going away. He could almost think again.

Was this it? Had he been broken? In answer, Fred staggered to his feet.

He had no idea what to do. He had nowhere to go for help. He thought of going to his owner, Master Thomas. But he was the one who had sent him to Covey in the first place! But if he stayed, Covey might kill him. Surely Fred's owner wouldn't want to see his "property" destroyed.

Covey was far off in the field. Fred watched him closely. When the slave breaker was looking the other way, Fred started to run. He was worn out and bleeding, but he forced himself to run faster and faster.

"Come back! Come back!" screamed Covey. But Fred didn't stop. Fred ducked into the woods. Covey wouldn't be able to follow him there.

It took Fred five hours to make it all the way to his owner's farm.

Master Thomas looked shocked. His slave was covered with dirt and blood from head to foot. Fred told him what had happened. He said that Covey would kill him if he went back to the farm.

"Nonsense," answered Thomas coldly. He told Fred that he was lazy, not sick. "You belong to Mr. Covey for one year, and you must go back to him, come what will. And if you don't go immediately home, I'll get hold of you myself."

Go back? Fred could barely stand. "But, sir," he protested, "I am sick and tired, and I cannot get home tonight."

Master Thomas at last agreed to let the bloody boy stay overnight. But he would have to leave for Covey's in the morning.

The next day he hiked back to Covey's farm. Just as he arrived at the farm, Covey jumped out. He had been hiding behind a fence, waiting for him. He had a whip in his hand.

Fred ran again. He made it to the forest and lost Covey in the dense brush. Covey returned to his house, cursing Fred loudly. Fred waited. But Covey did not return. Fred waited all day. He was starving. Covey knew that he would have to come in for food sometime. It seemed that Covey was willing to wait.

That night Fred sat in the pitch-black forest, listening. He heard footsteps.

Covey?

He held his breath, not making a sound. The man came closer. It was Sandy, a fellow slave!

Fred came out of hiding. He told Sandy what had happened. Sandy tried to comfort him. He said he was on his way to visit his wife. His wife was a free woman. She lived in her own little house. She could give him something to eat.

Fred gratefully agreed. He knew that Sandy was risking his own life to help him. If Covey found out that Sandy had fed him, he would beat him just as badly as he would beat Fred.

Sandy and his wife gave him food and shelter, and listened kindly to the teenager's tale of woe.

At last Fred was able to sleep. In the morning he felt strong, rested. There was nothing he could do. He had to go home. But he made up his mind. Covey had tried to break his spirit. He had almost succeeded. Fred would never allow this. The next time Covey attacked him, he would defend himself.

Hitting a white man—even in self-defense—

was a serious crime. A black man could be hanged for much less. Still, Fred told himself he would not be broken. He would fight.

It was Sunday. He headed for Covey's farm. As Fred entered the gate, Covey and his wife came out. They were going to church. Fred steeled himself for Covey's attack. But Covey smiled at him! He asked how Fred was. And kept walking.

Fred realized that Covey believed Sunday was a holy day. Covey would punish him tomorrow.

The next morning Covey ordered Fred to feed the horses. As he climbed up into the stable loft, Covey crept into the barn. He grabbed Fred's leg and pulled him onto the floor. He tried to tie up Fred's legs. But Fred sprang free. He grabbed Covey around the neck. Every time Covey tried to throw him down, he threw Covey down instead.

Covey was amazed. He began to shake. "Are you going to resist, you scoundrel?" he cried.

Fred stared Covey right in the eye. "Yes, sir," he replied.

Covey began to scream for help. His cousin Hughes came running in. Now it was two against one. But when Hughes rushed at Fred, the boy hit him so hard he doubled over.

Covey was breathing hard and could barely speak. He couldn't believe Fred had resisted him. Fred told Covey he had treated him like an animal. He wouldn't stand for it anymore.

There was a large stick lying near the door. Covey tried to drag Fred toward it, so he could beat him. But Fred threw Covey down again. Thanks to all that heavy work in the field, Fred's muscles had become strong. He had grown to be over six feet tall and broad-shouldered. Covey was no match for him.

Now another one of Covey's slaves happened to walk by. Covey ordered Bill to hold Fred down.

"*What* shall I do, Master Covey?" asked Bill, pretending not to understand.

"Take hold of him! Take hold of him!" yelled Covey.

But Bill said he had to get to work.

"This is your work," yelled Covey, "take hold of him."

But Bill said it wasn't his job to help whip Frederick, and he walked on.

The fight went on for two hours. Fred continued to defend himself. Covey was bleeding and breathing hard. He was also furious. None of his slaves would help him.

At last he saw it was no use. Letting go, he said, "Now, you scoundrel, go to your work. I would not have whipped you half so hard if you had not resisted."

Covey had not succeeded in whipping Fred at all. Fred had won!

The Escape

Fred had hit a white man. He was sure he would be killed. But Covey never told a soul.

Covey made his living "breaking" slaves. He didn't want anyone to know that Fred had dared to fight back. Besides, Fred had won. If word got around about that, Covey would be out of business.

The fight with Covey was a turning point in Fred's life. He had stood up for himself. For the first time, he felt powerful and confident.

He told himself that he would never be whipped again. He spread the word. Anyone who tried to whip him had better kill him. Because he would defend himself with all his might.

The long months with Covey had finally come to an end. On Christmas Day, in 1834, Frederick, almost seventeen years old, left Covey's farm. He had been "rented" by a new master, Mr. William Freeland.

Mr. Freeland was not as strict as Covey had been. Fred had a chance to read again, and to think. He could only think about one thing: freedom.

He had just endured a long and terrible punishment for disobedience. But he had come out stronger, and even more determined to fight against slavery.

He began by setting up another secret school for his fellow slaves. Besides reading and writing, he used the school meetings to talk about an even more dangerous subject. He talked to his fellow slaves about running away.

If he was caught, he knew, he could be imprisoned, or shipped off to the Deep South. From the Deep South there was even less chance of escape. The trip north was very far. Frederick felt he would then be a slave for life. But he saw no other way out. He would have to take this risk.

He learned that his five students all felt the same way. They were eager to go with him.

One of his students was Sandy, the man who had given him shelter from Covey. If Sandy could get north, his free wife could meet him there. Then they could be together all the time.

Fred worked out a plan. They would steal a canoe and paddle out into the Chesapeake Bay. They would travel the first seventy miles by water. Then they would try to make the rest of the way by land.

Now came the time for Fred to use his writing skill. Fred wrote fake passes for each slave. The passes said:

This is to certify that I, the undersigned, have given the bearer, my servant, full liberty to go to Baltimore to spend the Easter holidays.

The slaves packed food for the trip and hid it. They were all set.

Fred's plan was to make their escape that Saturday. All week long the slaves had to pretend that nothing unusual was about to happen. If the plan failed, Fred would feel responsible for ruining the lives of all of his men.

Sandy was having nightmares. He was scared of being caught. He decided to drop out of the group.

On Saturday morning Fred and his men went to work in the fields, as always. The slaves were spreading manure. Fred's heart was pounding hard. Suddenly Fred had a horrible thought.

He turned to Sandy and said, "Sandy, we are betrayed! Something has just told me so."

"Man, that is strange," answered Sandy. "But I feel just as you do."

Fred didn't know why, but he was sure they were about to be caught.

The horn blew. The field hands headed for the

house for breakfast. When Fred got to the house, he heard hoofbeats. In the distance he saw four white men galloping toward the farm.

It is indeed all over with us, he thought. We are surely betrayed.

One of the men asked Fred where Mr. Freeland was. Fred told them that his master was in the barn. The men galloped off.

Now three constables galloped into the front yard. They quickly got off their horses. The first group of men returned with Mr. Freeland. They all headed toward the kitchen where Fred stood.

Mr. Freeland told Fred to come out. He said there were some people here who wanted to speak with him. The other men surrounded Fred and tied him up with a rope.

Next they caught John Harris and tied him up as well. One of the men said, "Perhaps we had now better make a search for those protections, which we understand Frederick has written for himself and the rest."

They knew about Fred's passes! If they found them, he realized, they would have proof of his plot to escape.

Just then, John's brother Henry came out of the barn. The men went back outside and stopped him. They were ready to tie him up for being part of the plan to escape as well. "Cross your hands," ordered the constable.

"I won't," Henry said.

Two constables pointed pistols at Henry's head. They told him to cross his hands or they would blow his head off.

"Shoot me, shoot me!" cried Henry. "You can't kill me but once. Shoot, shoot, and be damned! I won't be tied!"

All the men gathered round and began to beat the poor slave. He couldn't defend himself. Fred looked away. But then he realized something. The fight was distracting the constables. As the men bound Henry with rope, Fred inched back toward the kitchen fire. Still looking forward, he carefully pulled his pass out of his pocket. Silently, he dropped it into the flames.

But each of the other men still had his pass. If the constables went ahead with their search, they were sunk. Luckily, the fight with Henry had distracted everyone. For the time being, they forgot to search for the passes!

The constables tied the prisoners to their horses. They made them march to prison. The whole town gathered to watch as the prisoners trudged by. Some cried out that Fred should be hanged. Others yelled that he should be burned or skinned alive.

Fred was tied to Henry. The slaves had been lucky enough to keep their passes hidden so far, but they would certainly be searched when they got

55

to the jail. When the constables weren't looking, Henry muttered to Fred, "What shall I do with my pass?"

"Eat it," Fred told him quietly. Fred whispered to the other men to eat their passes as well! Then he told them not to admit to a thing. After all, now the constables had no proof.

The poor men were dragged through the dust for fifteen miles. They were locked up in the Easton jail.

Now Master Thomas arrived and questioned them. He told Fred that he knew all about the escape plot. He had hard evidence.

"But we have not run away," argued Fred. "Where is the evidence against us? We were quietly at our work."

But it was no use. The men had been betrayed. But by whom? Fred never found out. All the men had a hunch. It was a suspicion they didn't want to believe. They suspected their old friend Sandy. Maybe he had been so frightened that he went to the master. Perhaps he hoped that by betraying the plot he would escape punishment himself.

Suddenly a loud group of slave buyers stormed into the prison. These men always hung around jails, looking for slaves they could buy cheap. If a slave had committed a crime, the slave's owners might sell the slave cheap. The slave buyers shook the prisoners and felt them all over. All the time, the slave buyers were laughing. They taunted the men. The prisoners didn't say a word.

Several days later everyone but Fred was released from jail. The rest would not be punished.

Fred was glad that the others had been let go. But now he was totally alone. A week crawled by. Then Master Thomas came back.

Fred knew what was coming. Master Thomas would sell him to someone in the Deep South. Fred was sure that all his dreams were about to come to an end. The struggle to read and write—what good had that done him? He was sure his mission was over.

In his despair, he could hardly focus on what Master Thomas was saying. Master Thomas began by talking about what a terrible troublemaker Fred was. But now he was saying something else. He was sending him back to Baltimore and his brother Hugh!

Free At Last!

Frederick was back in Baltimore again. He had been away for three years. A lot had changed. For one thing, Tommy had grown up. As a little boy, he had been glad to play with Freddy. Now Tommy wanted nothing to do with this *slave*. He treated Frederick coldly and didn't like to be seen with him.

Mr. Auld put Frederick to work in his shipyard. Since he was black, he had to serve every white worker. He had to follow every order. Often, the carpenters all shouted to him at once.

As Fred ran from one man to the next, the white men cursed him. Sometimes the carpenters hit him. Fred remembered his fight with Covey. He had vowed that he would always defend himself. He stuck to his pledge. Every time he was hit, he hit back.

For the white carpenters, this was something new. A slave who hit back? The men were shocked.

One day four carpenters, armed with bricks and spikes, attacked Fred from all sides. He was badly outnumbered. But Fred fought as hard as he could. Then someone hit him in the head with a spike and he fell.

The men began to kick him viciously. Fred lay still, trying to gather his strength.

All this time, fifty or so white carpenters were standing around, watching. "Kill him!" they shouted. "Knock his brains out! He struck a white person!"

Fred struggled to all fours. Then one man kicked Fred in the eye. He was nearly blinded.

Finally the men stopped. They left him lying there.

When Master Auld heard what had happened, he was furious. He took Fred to see a judge. He told Fred that they would find the men who had done this. They would have them arrested.

But the judge would do nothing to the white men. None of the carpenters was ever punished.

Frederick was twenty now. Again, he made up his mind to try for freedom. What could be worse than this?

Still, he had many friends in Baltimore. He was close with many slaves. He didn't want to leave them behind.

Fred had formed a secret club for blacks. The

club met in a shack in a deserted part of town called Happy Alley. Sometimes they gave parties. At one party, Fred had met a girl.

Her name was Anna Murray. She was five years older than he was. She worked as a maid for a rich French family. Anna was a free woman. Fred thought she was serious, strong, and practical. Perhaps it was this practical nature that appealed to him the most. Fred had become a fiery, passionate young man. He felt he had to defeat slavery all by himself. This woman's quiet strength was comforting to him.

Fred began to court Anna. He was falling in love. Then one day he asked Anna to marry him. She happily agreed.

But it wasn't time to celebrate yet. He was still a slave. He was in no position to marry anyone. First, he would have to escape. He would flee to New York. If he could make it, he would send for her. Since she was a free woman, she could travel to New York to join him.

But if he didn't make it . . . he would probably never see Anna again. But Fred and Anna agreed. He would take the chance.

Fred had worked out a new plan. This time he would try to escape alone. One of his friends was a free black sailor. Blacks who had been freed by their owners had to carry proof that they were free.

The proof was known as free papers. The papers listed the person's name and what they looked like.

Free blacks often lent their free papers to other slaves, to help them escape. Once the slaves had made it north, they would send back the papers. The free blacks who did this were risking their own freedom to help another. If a free black was found without his papers, he would be in serious trouble.

Fred did not match the description in his borrowed free papers. But it was the best he could do. He would dress as a sailor—and pray.

He decided that he would try to escape by train. The biggest problem was getting a ticket. At the ticket window, blacks were questioned carefully. They would study his free papers. He could be arrested immediately.

So Frederick arrived at the station just as the train was pulling out. The ticket master didn't have time to question him. He jumped aboard the moving car.

Back then, blacks were not allowed to ride with the white passengers. Fred made his way to the "Negro car."

First the conductor collected all the white people's tickets. At last the conductor came into the Negro car. He was coming closer and closer to Frederick. Soon it would be his turn.

The conductor looked down at Frederick. He

asked to see Frederick's papers. Frederick showed him the papers he had borrowed from the sailor. If the conductor studied these papers closely, Frederick's life would be over.

The conductor glanced at the papers and handed them back. He went on his way. Fred had made it!

But Frederick wasn't free yet. It was a long trip. He had to ride two trains and a ferry. He could be caught at any moment.

There were many close calls. Once, he saw a man staring at him. It was a blacksmith from Baltimore. The man knew him and knew that he was a slave. Their eyes met. But the man said nothing. The blacksmith had decided not to turn him in.

Twenty-four hours later Frederick arrived in New York. It was an amazing feeling. He was on free soil! As he walked around the crowded streets, everything he saw filled him with wonder. It was as if he were seeing all life had to offer for the first time.

Years later Frederick would write, "I felt as one might feel upon escape from a den of hungry lions."

But he still wasn't out of danger. Fred had no money, no friends, nothing to eat, and nowhere to sleep. At any moment someone might return him to Baltimore and collect a big reward.

But a few hours after he had arrived, he ran

into someone he knew. It was another runaway slave. The man called himself William Dixon.

William gave Frederick some scary news. There were spies everywhere. He couldn't go near the docks. They would look for him there. He shouldn't stay in a boarding house. They would search there as well. Dixon himself had almost been captured many times.

Frederick wanted to know more. But Dixon was scared to be around another wanted man. He hurried on his way.

That night Frederick slept in a barrel. He was starving. His excitement at being free was beginning to fade.

The next day Frederick stood on a street corner. He had no idea what to do next. Then a sailor approached him. Frederick was still wearing his sailor costume. The sailor asked if Frederick needed help. Could Frederick trust him?

Frederick decided that he had no choice. He told the sailor that he had run away. The sailor let Frederick stay in his house that night. The next morning he took him to see a man named Mr. David Ruggles.

It turned out that Mr. Ruggles was a conductor on the underground railroad that Fred had always heard about. That meant his house was a "station," a hideout for runaways on their way farther north. He hid Frederick in his house.

Frederick sent word to his fiancée, Anna. Come at once!

Anna rushed to New York. When she arrived, the couple went to a reverend friend of Mr. Ruggles's. Frederick had no money to pay the reverend. But Reverend Pennington understood. He was a runaway slave himself! He was happy to marry the young couple, free of charge.

There was no time for a honeymoon. It wasn't safe for the newlywed couple to stay in New York a minute longer. Kidnappers were probably closing in on Frederick already. In Baltimore Frederick had slaved in the shipyards as a caulker. That meant that he sealed up cracks in ships.

Mr. Ruggles suggested they flee to New Bedford, Massachusetts. New Bedford was a busy seaport. Maybe Frederick could find more caulking work there.

Frederick and Anna hurried straight from the reverend to the steamboat, the *John W. Richmond*. Black passengers were not allowed to go below deck to the safety of the cabins. Frederick and Anna spent the rainy night fighting the cold and trying to sleep. But they didn't mind too much. They were starting a new life. They had both been through much worse.

The important thing was to leave slavery far, far behind.

A New Life

A free black man named Nathan Johnson met the young couple in New Bedford. He put them up in his house. He loaned Frederick some money. He also advised Frederick that he had better change his name.

At the time Nathan was reading a novel called *The Lady of the Lake*. In the book there was a Scottish character he really liked called Douglass. He suggested this name. Frederick agreed.

He had been born Frederick Augustus Washington Bailey. For the rest of his life he would be Frederick Douglass. It was a name that would go down in history.

With his new name and new clothes, Frederick went to the wharves to look for work. On his way there, he saw a house with a large pile of coal in front. He knocked and asked if they needed someone to put the coal away.

"What will you charge?" the woman of the house asked.

"I will leave that to you, madam."

The woman answered, "You may put it away."

Frederick worked fast. When he was done, the woman gave him two silver half-dollars. Frederick was thrilled. He had earned his first money as a free man. The money he earned was his and his alone.

But New Bedford wasn't paradise. In Baltimore Frederick had learned a trade. He was a good caulker. But the white caulkers in New Bedford said they would quit if a black man were hired. Frederick couldn't practice his trade. He had to take whatever odd jobs he could find, like carrying out garbage or sawing wood. Anna had to go back to work as a maid.

Everywhere he went, Frederick brought along something to read. He wanted to educate himself more and more.

One of the papers he read was called *The Liberator*. The editor of the paper was a famous abolitionist, William Lloyd Garrison. Garrison wrote powerful speeches against slavery. Frederick eagerly read everything Garrison wrote.

Frederick began to go to anti-slavery meetings. His heart pounded as he heard people talk about the evils of the slave system.

He still feared that he would be arrested at any

minute. But other blacks in New Bedford told him not to worry. They all stuck together, they said. His secret was safe.

A year later, at the age of twenty-one, Frederick became a father. His daughter Rosetta was born on June 24, 1839. Frederick didn't know his own birthday. He would make sure Rosetta always knew hers. Frederick prayed that she would always be free.

On October 2, 1840, Frederick and Anna celebrated a second birthday. Lewis Henry was born.

One day Frederick heard about a big antislavery meeting being held near his home. William Garrison himself would be there!

Frederick was twenty-two now, and beginning to feel restless. He didn't want to spend his whole life as a handyman in New Bedford. He decided to travel to the meeting.

Here he was surrounded by a vast sea of white faces. All his life white men had been his tormentors. But many of these men were talking about how to end slavery. Not all of them. Some of the crowd had come to heckle the speakers. Some of the men were definitely *for* slavery.

Then Fred saw one of the white men, William Coffin, coming toward him. Mr. Coffin knew Frederick from New Bedford. Would Frederick get up and say a few words? he asked. He could tell the audience about his life as a slave.

Frederick was very nervous. But he agreed. He stood in front of the large hall. He began to tremble. When he started to speak, he stammered badly. He could barely stand up straight.

All his life he had been taught that white people were his superiors. He wasn't supposed to address them directly. And here he was being asked to lecture to a huge crowd of over 500 white people!

Then he began to talk about his life as a slave. He began to talk about the awful injustice he had seen. Here was his chance to tell his story. He stood up straighter. The words began to pour out.

Frederick had a deep and powerful voice. As he spoke, his eyes flashed. His moving speech soon overpowered the convention.

When he was done, William Garrison jumped to his feet. He said that Frederick had given one of the greatest speeches he had ever heard. Garrison called to the crowd. Would they ever let Frederick be stolen back into slavery?

"No!" the crowd roared back.

Would they protect him as a brother?

The crowd thundered its reply: "Yes!"

After the meeting, another man came over to Frederick. His name was Mr. John Collins. He worked for a group fighting slavery. Mr. Collins said he had been awed by Frederick's speech. Would Mr. Douglass be willing to work for his group? They would pay him to speak at meetings full-time!

It was hard to believe. He could be paid to speak! Frederick agreed.

But his friends in New Bedford were shocked at the news. They warned Frederick that the danger was tremendous. He would be telling everyone that he was a runaway slave. Word would get back to his owners. They would come to get him.

But Frederick thought about his people. Millions were still suffering as slaves while he lived free. He had to do something to help. Uncle Lawson had once told him that God meant him to do great work. Maybe it was time for that great work to begin.

Frederick began to give special lectures in small towns all over Massachusetts. The people who came to the lectures weren't friendly. All his life Frederick had dreamed of living in the northern states where blacks were free. He was finding that blacks here were free, but not from prejudice.

Frederick was usually introduced as a runaway piece of Southern property. Many people came just to see if a black man could really give a speech. They were sure that he couldn't.

But Frederick spoke beautifully. He used his deep, rolling voice to drive home his points.

Most of the people in his audiences didn't want to believe that a slave could speak so well. "He's never been a slave," people yelled out.

They insisted that Frederick was some kind of hoax. He was too well educated, they said. How could he possibly claim that he had never spent a day in school?

As word spread about his speeches, the problem grew worse. It looked as if Frederick's talks would be of no use. No one believed him! Finally, Frederick's employers asked him to publish his story as a book. He would have to give all the details of his life as a slave, as proof that his story was true.

But that would mean he would be advertising his escape. A book would tell his owners where he was. Publishing a book would be ten times more dangerous than giving a speech—for it would reach many more people.

But Frederick was determined to do whatever he could to fight slavery. He agreed to write down his story.

During the winter of 1844 to 1845 Frederick, now twenty-seven, devoted all of his time to his book. He would use the letters he once had chalked on fences to write the story of his life.

Frederick wrote day after day, month after

month. In simple words he told the nation what it was like to be a slave. He wrote about his mother, Grandmamma, Master Thomas, Miss Sopha. Many of the events were hard for him to write about. The pain was very fresh in his mind.

His book was called *Narrative of the Life of Frederick Douglass, An American Slave*. When he was done, he showed it to his bosses.

One man told him that the book would lead directly to his arrest. "Throw it in the fire," he warned.

Frederick knew the man was right. He had revealed everything in his book except the way he escaped and the names of people who had helped him to flee. But Frederick believed his book could help his people. So he went ahead and published it.

Many people who read Frederick's book were amazed and upset. Living in the North, people could put the problem of slavery out of their minds.

Critics who reviewed Frederick's book were also greatly impressed. Frederick's story soon became a bestseller. Within five years over 30,000 copies were sold. The book was translated into French and Dutch. The runaway slave had become a famous author!

"Notice! Frederick Douglass Will Lecture!"

Frederick had time to lecture again. But his book had put him in great danger. Now his owners knew where he was. The anti-slavery newspapers printed the time and place of each of his speeches. Kidnappers would know just where to find him. But he kept giving speech after speech.

Usually, he had to travel alone to give his talks. Travel for blacks was still hard, even in the free states. Blacks always had to ride in the worst part of the ship or train.

But Frederick had never been one to easily give in to rules he knew were wrong. He wanted to fight injustice against blacks everywhere. Wherever he went, he sat down in the "whites only" section.

"What are you doing in this car?" one train conductor demanded.

Frederick told him he was just riding the train like everyone else.

The conductor ordered him to switch seats. Frederick thanked him, but said he was happy with *his* seat. The conductor left. He soon returned with four or five other men. They grabbed Frederick and tried to pull him out of his seat by force. Frederick held onto his seat with all his might. The men pulled him to his feet, but they ripped out the train's seat as well!

In some Northern states Frederick succeeded in getting companies to change their ways. After a few years the New England trains began letting blacks ride with whites.

Frederick's troubles didn't end when he arrived at his destination. Many towns he visited wouldn't let him use the town hall or church to hold a meeting. They wouldn't let him into any of their houses or even the marketplace.

So Frederick would walk through the town ringing a bell. As he walked he loudly called, "Notice! Frederick Douglass, recently a slave, will lecture on American Slavery, this evening at seven o'clock."

Frederick would tell people to come to the public square. Usually only a few people showed up. But then Frederick would start to talk. His magical voice drew in the passersby.

"I appear this evening as a thief and a robber," Frederick often began by saying. "I stole this head, these limbs, this body from my master, and ran off with them!"

Who was this tall black man who spoke so powerfully, so beautifully? Soon a small curious crowd would gather. Then more people stopped to see what was going on. Frederick ended up addressing crowds of thousands.

Now the town leaders had no choice. They would let him move the huge crowd into the town hall.

In 1843 the abolitionists announced that they would try to hold one hundred meetings during the year. The meetings were scheduled all over the Northern states. Frederick spoke at every meeting.

Often, his speeches made people angry. There were some whites in the North who believed in slavery. They didn't like hearing a black man say that slavery was wrong.

In Indiana Frederick spoke outdoors to a large crowd. Suddenly a mob of angry whites rode in on horseback. The mob attacked Frederick and the other speakers with clubs. He was knocked to the ground and kicked again and again.

The mob got back on their horses and rode away. Frederick lay on the ground, unconscious. His right hand was broken. He would never have full use of it again.

By now Frederick was used to being attacked. As soon as he was well enough, he went back to giving speeches.

He kept hearing scary rumors, though. People said that his life was in danger.

Finally, his friends convinced him. For his own safety, they said, he must leave the country. It meant being apart from his wife, Anna, and his young children. But he had no choice. His friends bought him a ticket on the steamer *The Cambria*. In 1845 Frederick set off for England.

He had to stay away for two long years. While he was in England, a great deal was going on back home.

The South felt that the North, with its strong industry, was getting too powerful. What if the Northern states made them give up slavery? Southern farmers believed it would destroy their economy to lose the slave laborers they didn't have to pay.

Eventually the U.S. defeated Mexico in war and added over a million square miles of land to the Union. Southern leaders began a campaign to spread slavery to this new territory.

Frederick was far away in England, but he was keeping busy. He gave fiery talks against slavery. In America blacks now called him the Great Frederick. But many whites still spoke of him only with great contempt. In England, at least, white people treated him as the hero he was.

Many leading politicians came to see him. He met a lot of famous people, such as the writer Hans Christian Andersen. He made many new friends.

Some of Frederick's new friends in England were rich. Two wealthy sisters, Ellen and Anna Richardson, offered to buy him out of slavery! They wrote to his former master.

Master Hugh Auld demanded 150 pounds sterling ($700 in American money). The money was sent. Papers were signed. Frederick was finally free!

He returned to America at once. At last he could be with his wife and children.

Frederick had a new plan. His book had given him the idea. He would start his own newspaper. The newspaper would tell about the fight to stop slavery.

First he moved his family to Rochester, New York. He didn't want his paper to compete with the abolitionist newspapers already printed in Massachusetts.

Frederick called his paper *The North Star*. Travelers can find out which way north is by locating the

North Star in the sky. In the same way, he hoped his paper would help lead slaves to the North—and freedom.

Frederick didn't just *write* about freedom. He turned his house into a station on the underground railroad. Now he was a conductor. He could help runaway slaves just as Mr. Ruggles had once helped him.

Frederick once hid thirty runaways in two weeks. The escaped slaves hid in the house during the day. Once night fell, the slaves could continue on their way north.

Frederick also began to campaign to open Rochester's public schools to blacks. The school for black children was on the other side of town. Frederick's sons and daughters would have to hike for miles each day. He wrote powerful editorials in his paper. He gave speech after speech. And he managed to get a hearing with the Rochester Board of Education.

By now, Frederick was one of the world's most convincing speakers. He persuaded the Board of Education that he was right. The Board made its ruling. From now on, Rochester's schools would not keep blacks and whites apart.

Frederick had won a small battle. But he longed for much greater changes. In the South blacks were still slaves. And nowhere in America were blacks treated as equals. Prejudice was still everywhere. Blacks didn't even have the right to vote.

Frederick was beginning to believe that speeches and articles weren't enough. It might take a war to free his people. He didn't know it yet, but that war was coming.

Civil War

Thanks to people like Frederick Douglass, abolitionists were gaining power. They had been fighting slavery for over thirty years. All through the North, more and more people now believed that slavery must be stopped.

But the South wasn't giving up. The slave owners said they wanted *more* slave-owning states, not fewer!

Parts of the United States hadn't been divided into states yet. The South had been trying to claim these territories as extra slave states.

Southern politicians also argued for new laws to protect slavery. In 1850 Congress passed such a law. The law was a compromise between the North and the South. The South allowed California, a new state, to be slave-free. In return, the North went along with a law that said runaway slaves, if caught, must be returned to their owners.

As a result of this law, many of Frederick's closest friends had to flee to Canada. Many former slaves were not so lucky. After years of freedom, they were hunted down and brought back to the Deep South. Frederick was even more determined to fight against slavery.

"This Fourth of July is yours, not mine," he told a crowd sadly in 1852. *"You* may rejoice, I must *mourn."* He reminded the crowd that the holiday celebrated freedom for all in this new land. But African-Americans were still not free.

Violence between abolitionists and slave catchers was breaking out all over the North. It seemed that the country was moving closer to war.

On the night of October 16, 1859, Frederick was in the middle of a speech to a huge crowd in Philadelphia. Suddenly the announcement was made that a slave rebellion was under way. A small group of men—white and black—had seized several government buildings in Harpers Ferry, Virginia. The man leading the rebellion was a white man called Captain John Brown. A mass of militiamen surrounded Brown's men. The militiamen led by Lieutenant Colonel Robert E. Lee quickly overpowered the handful of rebels. Many of Brown's soldiers died in the battle. Brown himself was arrested, tried, and hanged.

But his attack was not in vain. It had stirred up the country. More than ever, it seemed like

North and South were becoming two different countries.

In 1860 four people were running for President of the United States. One of these four believed that slavery was wrong. He didn't believe that the government had the right to abolish slavery in Southern states where it already existed. But he did believe that slavery should be kept out of all new territories.

His name was Abraham Lincoln. His views were so hateful to the South that some Southern states made a wild threat. If Lincoln were elected, they said, the South would *secede*. That meant they would drop out of the country. To keep its slaves, the South would form its own government!

Frederick believed in Lincoln. He thought if Lincoln were elected President, his people had a chance to be free. He spoke to every white person who would listen. He prayed that Lincoln would win.

Abraham Lincoln did win. And the South carried out its threat. State after state seceded.

The South had formed a new government called the Confederate States of America. A man named Jefferson Davis became the South's new President.

War didn't break out right away. For six months President Lincoln begged the Southern states to rejoin the Union. But he had no success.

He vowed he would hold the nation together, even if that meant war.

Meanwhile, all over the South, Southern soldiers were taking over U.S. government buildings and forts. In Charleston, South Carolina, there was a small group of Northern soldiers who continued to guard Ft. Sumter. Southern soldiers had them surrounded. But they refused to surrender.

At 4:30 in the morning on April 12, 1861, cannons boomed. Southern troops had opened fire on Ft. Sumter. The Civil War had begun.

The war did not begin well for the North. At Bull Run, Virginia, Confederate soldiers crushed the Union troops. Frightened by this first defeat, Northern generals spent months training and organizing a larger army. When they finally went back to battle, in 1862, they lost again.

Frederick was greatly troubled. Since the beginning, he felt that the purpose of the war should be to free the slaves. But no one in the government was saying this. In fact, some people in the government were saying just the opposite.

General George McClellan, head of the Northern army, warned slaves not to try to escape. "If any attempt is made by them to gain their freedom," the general announced, "it will be suppressed with an iron hand."

Northern troops were carrying out his orders.

They were returning runaway slaves to their masters!

Frederick pleaded for the North to stop returning slaves at once. In speeches and in his paper he pointed out that the Southern army was making its slaves work hard behind the lines for the Southern cause. If these slaves could be freed, there would be fewer slaves to help the enemy. Frederick also pleaded for the Northern army to let blacks fight for the Union.

Slowly, the Northern army began to take his advice. At first, blacks had only been used by the Union regiments as waiters. Now the army began to recruit blacks as laborers, digging trenches and handling other hard chores. It was a step forward. But they still wouldn't let the black men fight.

Frederick urged the army to change its policy. Black people wanted to fight this war more than anyone, he told them. They wanted to fight for their own freedom.

But the army refused. They told Frederick whites would never fight in an army with blacks. The officers said that if blacks were allowed to join the army, the white soldiers would all go home.

The bloody war dragged on and on. Thousands of men were dying on both sides. The North needed more soldiers desperately. Finally, in 1862, the army agreed to use blacks.

In the beginning, black soldiers weren't allowed to wear the regular blue uniforms. And they weren't allowed to rise to the rank of officer. But it was a start.

Frederick was forty-four years old. He was too old to fight as a foot soldier. But he was eager to serve as an officer. The army refused. White men would never take orders from a black officer, they said.

So Frederick kept working behind the lines. In his newspaper he printed articles urging young blacks to join the war.

"Men of color," he wrote, *"to arms!"*

Frederick's bold words inspired many. Over a hundred thousand young black men rushed to enlist. Frederick was proud of them all, but he was particularly proud of three soldiers. In New York State they had been the very first blacks to join the Union army. The soldiers were his sons. Charles, Lewis, and young Frederick had all gone off to war.

Black soldiers were taking a greater risk than any other soldiers in the Union army. There was no guarantee that the North would win. What would happen to them if the South took control of the country? Surely, the Southern government would execute any black who had dared to fight against a white. And if the North won? The Northern government was still promising to let the South keep its slaves.

Still, the black troops went into battle. They

soon proved to be brave soldiers. Word of their heroism spread rapidly throughout the country.

Now Frederick felt even more proud. For years slave owners had claimed that blacks were somehow worth less than whites. The black troops had proven them wrong in front of the whole country. They were standing up against their enemy, just as Frederick had once stood up against the slave breaker Edward Covey.

But Frederick also remained angry. The black troops faced greater dangers than white troops did. When the Southern army took a black soldier as a prisoner, they sold him into slavery. Sometimes they killed him.

This would never happen to a white prisoner. Both sides kept their white prisoners safe. But when black prisoners were killed, the Northern army did nothing.

Frederick felt responsible. He had sent many black boys off to war—including his own sons. He had to do something to protect them. He decided to go directly to Washington, D.C. He would make his complaint in person. He would try to see the President!

Would President Lincoln agree to see him? Frederick had no idea. He knew only that he had to try.

* * *

Frederick was in the White House, waiting to see the President. He could hardly believe it! Here he was, an ex-slave, trying to give advice to the head of a huge nation.

Frederick was shown into a large room. There was President Lincoln, sitting on a low armchair. Frederick noticed that the President's long legs stretched out far across the floor!

His name was announced—Frederick Douglass. President Lincoln's face lit up. He stood up. He held out his hand.

Frederick had been scared to meet such a powerful man. But something in Lincoln's manner put him at ease. The President seemed like a man he could trust.

Frederick began to explain who he was and why he had come. But the President interrupted him.

"I know who you are, Mr. Douglass. Sit down. I am glad to see you."

Frederick began his speech. He said that blacks no longer wanted to join the army. They felt that they weren't being treated fairly.

Frederick went on with all of his complaints. First, he wanted black soldiers to be paid the same wages as white soldiers. Second, when black prisoners were killed, the Northern army should respond. They should kill some of the Southern

prisoners in revenge. Third, black soldiers who proved particularly brave in battle should be rewarded with medals and promotions just as white soldiers were.

President Lincoln listened silently to all of Frederick's complaints. His face was grave.

Then he answered. Sadly, he told Frederick that there was still tremendous prejudice against his people, even in the North. It had been a long uphill battle, the President reminded him, just to get blacks into the army at all. He promised Frederick that he would try to give the black soldiers equal pay as soon as he could. But, he said, he was willing to compromise on equality in some cases now, for the sake of full equality later.

Frederick's second point, the President said, was a tough, painful problem. He said the army would have to find the Southern soldiers who had actually killed black prisoners. These soldiers would be punished. But he didn't believe in killing innocent Southern prisoners to punish the crimes of others.

Frederick didn't agree with the President. But he admired the man's kindness and strict moral code.

The President did agree to one of Frederick's suggestions. He promised to promote worthy black soldiers and make them officers.

Frederick was not satisfied by what the President had offered. But Lincoln's kindness had won his respect. In turn, he promised to recruit more black soldiers.

While Lincoln was passionately opposed to slavery, keeping the Union together was still his number one goal. After his meeting Frederick felt even more sure that the President cared deeply about the suffering of his people. And that gave him new hope.

It was September 22, 1862. The Civil War had raged for almost two terrible years. It wasn't close to being over. But for African-Americans, a tremendous victory was about to be won.

In Washington that morning President Lincoln was scheduled to make a special announcement. He was planning to say that all slaves must go free. It had been about a year since Frederick had first met with the President. Frederick was about to see a dream of his come true.

Throughout the nation people huddled near telegraph offices, waiting for the word. Frederick prayed that Lincoln would go through with his plan. But he also knew that just because Lincoln *said* all slaves were free, that didn't mean the South would listen. The North would still have to win the war. But it would be a great start. There were four million black men, women, and children living as slaves in the South. Maybe one day soon they could all go free!

Hours went by and still no news. Then a man rushed into the church. He was beaming. "It is coming!" he yelled. "It is on the wires!"

Then came the news. President Lincoln had abolished slavery! Even though Frederick had been expecting it, the news still felt unbelievable. He began to weep with happiness.

All day long the joyous crowd stayed and sang songs of freedom.

Come At Once!

Lincoln's announcement had been wonderful news. But it did not end the war. And if the North lost, the whole country could be turned over to the slave system.

One day Frederick got an urgent message. It was from the White House. The President needed his advice.

Frederick was a runaway slave. He had had to teach himself to read and write. And now he would be serving as an adviser to the nation's President!

The President told Frederick that he was disappointed. He had hoped his announcement would convince many slaves to run away to the North. Sadly, he said, "The slaves are not coming so rapidly and so numerous to us as I had hoped."

Frederick explained that slave owners worked hard to keep their slaves in ignorance. Probably, few slaves had heard about Lincoln's announcement.

"Well," said Lincoln, "I want you to set about devising some means of making them acquainted with it, and for bringing them into our lines."

Frederick tried to cheer up the President and suggested several plans. He said he could organize a special band of black men. They would travel into the Deep South and spread the word about Lincoln's announcement. He and the President talked for hours.

Frederick never allowed himself to believe the North would lose the war. His determination and enthusiasm must have inspired the President.

In 1864 President Lincoln faced another election. Again Frederick campaigned hard for Lincoln and again Lincoln won.

Frederick went to the inauguration ceremony. President Lincoln gave a speech. His speech was serious and somber. The country was still fighting a terrible war. Lincoln said that the nation was paying for its sins, the sin of slavery.

When the President finished his speech, Frederick clapped hard. He looked around at the crowd. He could tell that many people had not liked the speech at all. Frederick worried for his friend. There were many angry white people who wished the President dead. They were furious that Lincoln had said all slaves should go free.

That night a party was held at the White House. Frederick wanted to go and congratulate his friend President Lincoln. But no black had ever been to such a party. He didn't know if he would be allowed inside.

When Frederick got to the door, two policemen stopped him. They told him that no blacks could enter. Frederick answered that he was sure President Lincoln never said any such thing.

"I shall not go out of this building till I see President Lincoln," Frederick announced.

Guests were lining up behind him, waiting to get in. Still, the policemen refused to let him by. Then Frederick saw someone he knew. He asked the guest to get word to the President that he was waiting outside. Soon, a messenger returned and ordered the police to let Frederick through.

Inside he found the fanciest party he had ever seen. It was easy to spot the President. The tall man stuck way out of the crowd.

President Lincoln saw Frederick. He called to him loudly, making sure all the guests heard. "Here comes my friend Douglass."

He took Frederick's hand. "I am glad to see you. I saw you in the crowd today, listening to my speech. How did you like it?"

"Mr. Lincoln," Frederick answered, "I must not detain you with my poor opinion when there are thousands waiting to shake hands with you."

"No, no," said the President. "You must stop a little, Douglass. There is no man in the country whose opinion I value more than yours. I want to know what you think of it."

"Mr. Lincoln, that was a sacred effort."

Delighted, the President replied, "I am glad you liked it!"

Frederick moved on. He would never see the President again. He was home in Rochester one month later when the news came that Lincoln had been killed.

What Next?

Before Lincoln was shot, he saw the North win the war at last. For Frederick, the victory ended a lifetime of struggle. Finally slavery had been defeated.

What was next? Frederick had saved a few thousand dollars from the sales of his books. His children were all grown. He and Anna thought about buying a tiny farm and retiring to a quiet life.

Frederick thought about it, but not for long. He knew that his people's troubles were not over. And so, he told himself, his work was not over, either. The freed slaves were poor and uneducated. And they still could not vote.

Frederick set a new goal for himself. He would make sure every African-American had the right to vote.

He began to campaign in his old fashion, with letters, articles, and speeches. He was in for an unhappy surprise. Many of the white leaders of the anti-slavery movement were appalled by his new project. Freeing the blacks was one thing, they said. But the slaves were ignorant. How could they vote?

Besides, Frederick was told, the war had just ended. It was a bad time for blacks to demand more rights.

Frederick didn't agree. Without the right to vote, he said, blacks couldn't protect their new freedom. "If the Negro knows enough to fight for his country," Frederick wrote, "he knows enough to vote!"

On February 7, 1866, Frederick went to see the new President of the United States. This time he planned to speak about voting rights. He led a group of ten men, including his son Lewis. Unlike Lincoln, this President, Andrew Johnson, was not sympathetic to the cause of African-Americans. In fact, he had a special plan in mind for blocking Frederick's proposal.

Frederick and the group told the President why they had come. President Johnson answered with a forty-five-minute written speech. He said that former slaves were too angry at whites to be trusted with any political power. He said that at some point the ex-slaves should probably be sent back to Africa!

When the President finished his speech, he wouldn't let Frederick respond! Frederick saw that he had been tricked. The President's speech would be written up in all the morning papers, with no response from Frederick and his group. With no one to answer his arguments, the President might win many people to his side.

Frederick and the group huddled together after the meeting. They asked Frederick to write a reply as quickly as he could. There was no time to lose if Frederick wanted to make the newspapers' deadlines. Frederick threw together a response. The group rushed copies of his letter to newspaper offices.

Frederick's powerful words ran right next to the President's speech. People took notice.

The war had ravaged the South. That September, a special convention was held in Philadelphia. The purpose of the meeting was to make plans for helping the South get back on its feet.

One of the main topics at the convention would be whether to give blacks the right to vote. Frederick desperately wanted to attend as the delegate from Rochester. But Rochester was a city of over 60,000 white people. There were only 200 blacks, and they couldn't vote! How could Frederick, a runaway slave, hope to be elected by a city of whites?

Frederick was stunned by the results of the election. Rochester had chosen *him*! Frederick boarded a train for Philadelphia. He would be the only black delegate from the entire country.

This time, he thought, he didn't have to worry

about being thrown off the train for sitting in the white section! He would, however, face other problems.

During the trip a group of delegates approached him. They told Frederick that they all hoped he would not attend the meeting!

A black at the convention would make many whites furious. Frederick would hurt his own people's cause, they said.

Frederick listened quietly to the lengthy speech. He didn't say a word until it was over. He stared hard at the politicians. "Gentlemen," he said finally, "with all respect, you might as well ask me to put a loaded pistol to my head and blow my brains out, as to ask me to keep out of this convention, to which I have been duly elected."

Frederick's troubles were not over yet. The convention was scheduled to begin with a parade. The delegates would march two by two through Philadelphia. More delegates approached Frederick. They begged him not to march.

The crowds will grow violent, they warned him, if they see a black man marching arm in arm with whites. Besides, they said, no one will march with you.

Frederick told them that nothing would keep him from marching. But he couldn't help feeling panicked. Many of the delegates wouldn't even speak to him. Who would march with him?

Then, at the last minute, a New York delegate walked over to Frederick and shook his hand warmly. He asked Frederick if he would march with him. Relieved and grateful, Frederick agreed.

Huge crowds lined the Philadelphia streets as the delegates marched to their first meeting. The spectators cheered loudly. But they cheered loudest of all for the one black delegate, Frederick Douglass.

In the end, the convention agreed that black men should have the right to vote. Eventually, Congress agreed. An amendment to the Constitution was passed in 1870. Frederick had helped to win another enormous battle for his people.

If Frederick wanted to retire to a quiet life now, he wasn't given a chance. First he was asked to run the Freedmen's Savings Bank, a new bank for blacks. Over the next few years he would get even more impressive jobs. The U.S. government sent him as its representative to Santo Domingo. He rode there on an American man-of-war. This time he was not made to sleep out on the deck. The ship made the trip in *his* honor.

Next he was appointed U.S. Marshal for Washington, D.C. As a boy, Frederick had had no rights. He could be whipped whenever his white "owners" wanted. He could be held in jail for as long as his owners wanted. He couldn't even appear in court.

Now he had been appointed to manage the courts and jails of a whole district!

One day Frederick got a message from Maryland. His old master, Thomas Auld, was dying.

Frederick hadn't been home in fifty-six years. He still remembered how cruel the man had been. But to his own surprise, he found he still wanted to see him. Why?

In a way, Thomas had been one of Frederick's many stepfathers growing up. True, he had been an extremely mean and horrible man, but still, he was like a father to Frederick.

To this day, Frederick didn't know who his real father was. But all his life he had heard rumors that his father had been a white man. Not only that, some said his father was Thomas.

Thomas was in his eighties now, and sick with palsy. His hands shook badly. When Frederick entered the room, Thomas called out, "Marshal Douglass." Frederick had left Thomas as a slave in tattered rags. He was now a tall, striking man in a three-piece suit.

"Captain Auld," Frederick said.

They shook hands, and Thomas began to cry. To his own surprise, Frederick began to cry as well.

Then they began to talk about the past. Thomas told him that he had read Frederick's first book. When he read about himself, he felt bad. He said he hadn't known that Andrew had left Frederick's grandmother out in the woods.

What had Thomas thought when he ran away? Frederick asked.

"Frederick," Thomas said, "I always knew you were too smart to be a slave. And had I been in your place, I should have done as you did."

The old man was tired. Frederick was about to go. But then he turned for one last question. Did Thomas know when his birthday was?

Master Thomas didn't know the exact day. But he could tell him he was born in February, 1818. Frederick was a year younger than he thought!

Frederick lived to celebrate many more birthdays. He never stopped working to help his people get equal rights.

He didn't just work for blacks. Frederick believed that all men are created equal. And all women, too. Black men could now vote. But women—white and black—still didn't have voting rights. Frederick knew this was terribly wrong. He was one of the first men to join the women's movement. Whenever he could, he spoke at rallies for women's rights.

He also continued to work for the government. He advised many more presidents and served as the U.S. representative to Haiti.

At age seventy-eight, Frederick was still giving speech after speech. On the day of his death, he gave a fiery speech for women's rights. Later, at home in Anacostia Heights, D.C., he suffered a heart attack and died.

Over 25,000 people came to Frederick's funeral in Washington, D.C. Black and white, the mourners stood in the rain. They waited to say good-bye to their hero.

After the funeral, a train carried Frederick's coffin back to his earlier home of Rochester, New York. He was buried in the Mount Hope cemetery.

As it turned out, not even death could silence Frederick Douglass. That year, the book of his life story was printed again. Thousands more read his great words.

His writings and speeches are still being read today. He continues to teach the world that all human beings are created equal.

Highlights in the Life of

FREDERICK DOUGLASS

1818 In February Frederick Augustus Washington Bailey is born in Tuckahoe, Maryland. He is born a slave.

1825 His owner gives the seven-year-old Frederick to a Baltimore family as a gift.

1833 He is sent back to Tuckahoe and Master Thomas, a cruel man. Starving, the fifteen-year-old is often disobedient.

1834 Master Thomas sends Frederick to a slave breaker for a year. But Frederick fights back against the slave breaker and wins.

1836 Frederick organizes an escape attempt. But someone betrays him. He is thrown in jail. Master Thomas finally sends him back to Baltimore.

1838 Frederick flees disguised as a sailor. He makes it to New York City. He is free at last!

1841 Frederick is asked to speak at an anti-slavery meeting. He is nervous. But his powerful speech overwhelms the crowd. He is hired by William Garrison to speak against slavery.

1845 Frederick gives speech after speech. He speaks so well that people don't believe he was ever a slave. He risks his own freedom by publishing his life story. The book becomes a bestseller. Frederick is famous now. Too famous. He must flee to England for safety.

1847 Frederick returns from exile in England as a free man. He moves his family to Rochester, New York. He becomes a conductor on the underground railroad. And he starts his own newspaper, *The North Star.*

1861 The Civil War begins when a Southern army opens fire on Fort Sumter. Too old for battle himself, he fights for the right of blacks to join the Northern army.

1862 Frederick is in Boston on January 1 when word comes of President Abraham Lincoln's historic announcement. Lincoln has freed the slaves. But first, the North must win the war.

1864 President Lincoln sends for Frederick in August. He wants his advice on getting more slaves to run away.

1865 The North wins the war at last. The slaves can all go free.

1866 Frederick is the only black delegate elected to attend the post-war Philadelphia convention on reconstruction.

1877 President Rutherford Hayes makes Frederick the marshal of the District of Columbia. It is one of many important jobs Frederick will hold in the U.S. government.

1895 On February 20, Frederick dies at the age of seventy-eight. Over 25,000 people come to his funeral. They honor one of America's greatest heroes.